WHAT?
is
the Bible?

Scripture quotations are taken from the New King James Version unless otherwise noted.

ISBN: 978-1-947319-74-5

Cover and text layout design: Kristi Yoder

Printed in the USA

Published by:

TGS International
P.O. Box 355
Berlin, Ohio 44610 USA
Phone: 330.893.4828
Fax: 330.893.2305
www.tgsinternational.com

TGS001722

Table of Contents

Introduction

Many people today don't know much about the Bible. They may have seen Bibles in a store or at a garage sale, but they've never read one. They might have a vague impression of the Bible as an ancient book containing historical myths and outdated rules of morality. Other than that, they don't have a strong opinion about the Bible.

I suspect that if you're reading this booklet, you probably have a Bible and are thinking of reading it. Or maybe you've been reading a Bible and are looking for guidance to understand it better. In either case, I'd like to welcome you to the Bible, and in this booklet, spend some time introducing you to it.

I am delighted that you have chosen to read the Bible and that you want to understand it better. It is a wonderful book, and you have an exciting journey ahead of you.

1

A Story of Two Men

The Beginning

Once upon a time, only God existed. We don't know anything about this pre-time era except that God decided to create the heavens and the earth and everything in them (Colossians 1:16).

He placed a man and woman on earth to look after His new creation. God called the man Adam, and Adam called the woman Eve. God planted a beautiful garden of trees and plants where these two people would live. He placed everything they needed in the garden.

I'm going to tell you a little more about Adam and Eve because the Bible grew out of their story.

The First Adam

God created Adam before Eve. Adam then named all the animals as God brought them to him. It seems that during this process, Adam noticed that every animal he named had a mate. He began to look for a mate for himself, but was unable to find one that was like him.

God knew Adam needed a partner. He put Adam to sleep, took a rib from his side, and created a woman from it. When Adam woke up and saw Eve for the first time, he said, "This one at last is like me."[1]

Adam and Eve were good friends with God. Sometimes in the evening God would come down and talk with them in the garden. They had wonderful times together.

But God didn't force Adam and Eve to be His friends. He gave them a choice so they would be His friends because they wanted to. Even before He created Eve, God had planted two special trees in the garden. The first one He called the Tree of Life. The second one He called the Tree of the Knowledge of Good and Evil. He told Adam he could eat fruit from the first tree, but not from the second one. If he ate from the first tree, he would live

---

[1] Paraphrased from Genesis 2:23.

forever. If he ate from the second tree, he would die.[2]

Adam and Eve's paradise didn't last long. Unknown to them, Satan had rebelled against God and was forced out of heaven with his followers. The Bible doesn't tell us when this happened, but he came to earth, determined to get back at God by destroying Adam and Eve.

Soon after this, Adam and Eve met Satan in the garden, disguised as a serpent. He caught their attention with a question. "Is it really true that God said you may not eat from any of the trees in the garden?"[3]

Pointing to the Tree of the Knowledge of Good and Evil, Eve declared, "No. God told us we can eat from every tree in the garden except this one. He said that if we eat fruit from it or touch it, we will die."

Satan had their attention now, which was what he was after. He shook his head with just the right touch of skepticism on his face. "You won't die," he assured Eve. "You see, God knows that as soon as you eat fruit from that tree, you will become like Him. You will understand good and evil."

Eve remembered that God had called the tree the Tree of

[2] God allowed them to choose which tree they would eat from, but He did not allow them to eat from both. It had to be one tree or the other. You can't live forever and die at the same time.

[3] The Bible doesn't address the question of why Adam and Eve didn't seem surprised to hear a serpent talk.

the Knowledge of Good and Evil. She had wondered what good and evil were, but had never gotten a clear answer. Here was her chance to find out. She took a closer look at the tree. It was beautiful. Its leaves were a lush green, interspersed with luscious-looking fruit. Her mouth watered as she gazed at it.

She picked two of the fruit and brought one to Adam, who had been silently watching this whole scenario. "Let's eat it together," she suggested. Adam hesitated while Satan held his breath. Eve took a bite and closed her eyes in delight. "Ooh," she whispered. "It's good."

Adam looked at the fruit in his hand and thought of what God had said. Then he looked at Eve, who was ecstatically gobbling the rest of her fruit as if she couldn't eat it fast enough. He watched the juice drip from her chin. Then he lifted his hand and slowly took a bite.

Satan smiled. "Okay, God. Let's see what you make of this," he whispered. He knew he wouldn't need to wait long.[4]

You can read this story and what happened after it in the first few chapters of the book of Genesis, the first book in the Bible.

The Second Adam

The Old Testament is the history of Adam and Eve's family

---

[4] Author's note: The Bible doesn't give us much detail about how this all happened. My description pictures what I think could have taken place.

and the results of their sin. It tells us what they did with the knowledge they received when they disobeyed God.

But the story doesn't end there. God wanted to help humans find their way back to Him and restore the relationship Adam and Eve had lost. The New Testament tells us about Jesus, God's Son. It calls Him the second Adam because He was sinless and perfect like Adam had been before he sinned.

Jesus, God's Son, came to the earth about 2,000 years ago. He came to tell us more about God and to show us what God is like. He taught people about truth for three years. He showed them the power of God by healing the sick, casting out demons, and even bringing some dead people back to life.

The devil knew about Jesus' coming to earth, just as he had known about Adam and Eve. He knew Jesus had come to destroy the wall that stood between God and man. So the devil came to Jesus to tempt Him, just as he had tempted Adam and Eve some thousands of years before.

Jesus went into the wilderness after His baptism, and Satan met Him there. It was the first direct confrontation between the Son of God and the ruler of all evil. Jesus had been fasting for forty days, and He was hungry, so Satan attacked Him on that first. "If you're God's Son, turn these stones into bread so that you can eat." It was a direct challenge to Jesus, asking Him to use His special powers to prove

Himself the Son of God. (Satan loves the word *if*.)

But Jesus, like most Jews, had memorized large parts of the writings of Moses. Instead of paying attention to Satan's suggestions as Eve had, He quoted from Deuteronomy. "Man shall not live by bread alone, but by every word that proceeds from the mouth of God."

He didn't even bother defending His status as God's Son. It didn't matter what Satan thought of Him.

Satan didn't bother arguing either. Instead, he took Jesus to Jerusalem and set Him on top of the highest peak of the temple. "Okay," he said to Jesus, "if you really are God's Son as you claim, throw yourself down from here." Satan knew the Old Testament too, and he quoted it to Jesus. " 'He shall give His angels charge over you . . . in their hands they shall bear you up, lest you dash your foot against a stone.' "

Satan's sneer might have caused a lesser man to take his dare. But Jesus was the Son of God and far above such petty things. He answered calmly, "It is written again, 'You shall not tempt the Lord your God.' "

Satan had one more trick up his sleeve. He knew Jesus' goal was to bring the world back to God. So why not do it the easy way? He took Jesus to the top of a high mountain and showed Him the kingdoms of the world. "I will give all of them to you if you will kneel down and worship me," he promised.

It was a crowning insult. Jesus' eyes flashed fire at Satan's words. "Get out of here, Satan," He said sternly. "It is written, 'You shall worship the Lord your God, and Him only you shall serve.' "

Jesus did not give in to Satan's temptations. He passed the test and obeyed His Father rather than yielding to the evil pleasures the devil offered Him. As he had done to Eve, so the devil tried to use "truth" to trick Jesus. He even quoted Old Testament verses, taken out of context, to try to fool Him. But Jesus saw right through his trickery. He quoted truth from the Old Testament as answers. You can read this story in Matthew 4:1–11.

Jesus passed the test of obedience that Adam and Eve failed. Because of this, He was able to break down the wall that sin had placed between God and humans. As you read the Gospels in the New Testament, you will learn about the terrible price He paid to do it.

Jesus Christ is indisputably the key figure of the New Testament, as attested to by the following verses from the Bible:

- *Jesus said to him, "I am the way, the truth, and the life. No one comes to the Father except through Me"* (John 14:6).
- *Nor is there salvation in any other, for there is no other name under heaven given among men by which we must be saved* (Acts 4:12).

2

Why Would You Read the Bible?

I'm going to look at the story of Adam and Eve a little more. I want to offer some reasons from that story why you should read the Bible.

The Bible Tells Us About Sin

God's "rulebook" was the shortest one in history. It consisted of only one simple sentence. On the first day of Adam's life, God told Adam that He had placed the Tree of the Knowledge of Good and Evil in the middle of the garden. He said, "Of every tree of the garden you may freely eat; but of the Tree of the Knowledge of Good and Evil you shall not eat, for in the day that you eat of it, you shall surely die."

That was it. And God didn't have any other requirements that He would reveal later. Had Adam and Eve listened to this one very important instruction, God would never have needed to write the rest of the Bible. However, Adam and Eve disobeyed God and opened the floodgates for evil to invade the world.

The Bible tells us the story of the results of sin on the human family. It also tells us what God did to make it possible for us to find our way back to Him. The Bible is an open letter from God to all humanity, as well as a personal letter to you and me.

The Bible grew as God continued to give more information to His people. It took several thousand years for God to finish His letter.[1] He used at least forty writers throughout that time. It is interesting to watch His message develop in the Bible.

The Bible Teaches Us to Recognize Good and Evil

God created Adam and Eve innocent. They did not have or need the knowledge of good and evil. They had God to guide them, and as long as they obeyed the one rule He had given them, everything they did was good. But the devil persuaded

---

[1] Most sources will say 1,500 years. That depends whether the first parts of Genesis were handed down in writing or by oral tradition. Either could have been true.

them that God was depriving them of something desirable that they had a right to.

When Adam and Eve disobeyed God and ate the forbidden fruit, they lost their innocence. For the first time, they experienced the heavy weight of guilt. They learned that the knowledge of good and evil came through experiencing evil. It was a bitter discovery for them, and life was never the same again. The knowledge of evil opened the door for many temptations God had shielded them from. They had to start worrying about the possibility of doing evil, and life immediately became complex.

Even though we now have the knowledge of good and evil, it is not a complete knowledge. We have a conscience that helps us understand what is right and wrong, but it isn't perfect. Because our knowledge is not complete and our consciences are not perfect, God has given us the Bible. As we read it, it will provide us with a complete knowledge of what is good and what is evil.

The Bible Shows Us Truth

There are many ways to define and use truth. When the devil told Eve that having the knowledge of good and evil would make her become like God, his statement was partially true.[2] But he had a devious purpose. Because of his evil intentions,

---

[2] God agreed with this statement (see Genesis 3:22).

the devil did not tell Eve the whole truth, even though his words were true.

Life is very complicated, especially if people want to do what is right and believe the truth. Ever since Adam and Eve opened the door to the knowledge of good and evil, human beings have faced the challenge of needing to decide what is true and what is false. They have also needed to find a way to please God.

As God's list of expectations grew longer, people began to realize how hard it was to have the knowledge of good and evil, yet do only good things. Evil often seemed more attractive and easier to do than the good.

Furthermore, evil promised to bring fulfillment. But when people gave in and did evil, they felt guilty and deprived rather than happy and fulfilled. They became miserable and unhappy.

Some people tried hard to do what God wanted, but they failed over and over. They discovered they weren't good enough to please God. You may feel that way as well. Maybe you are reading the Bible to try to find your way out of the situation that resulted when Adam and Eve ate the forbidden fruit.

God has an answer for you!

He gave us the Bible to help us out of our dilemma. It tells us about actions, desires, and habits that are wrong and will displease God. It tells us what truth is and what it isn't. It tells us how to regain the relationship with God that Adam and Eve had at the beginning. Because God wants us to be His children as Adam and Eve were, we can trust the Bible, knowing that God is telling us the truth with good intentions. The Bible shows us how to serve God.

We will come back to this in more detail later. But to keep it simple for now, the Old Testament gives us the history and background I just gave you in the last paragraphs. It defines the word *sin* while the New Testament provides the answer to the human dilemma created by sin.

One of the New Testament writers said it this way. (This is a paraphrase, to make it easier to understand what I am trying to say.)

> [21] Is there a conflict, then, between God's law and God's promises? Absolutely not! If the **[Old Testament]** law could give us new life, we could be made right with God by obeying it. [22] But the Scriptures declare that we are all prisoners of sin, so we receive God's promise of freedom only by believing in Jesus Christ. [23] Before the way of faith in Christ was available to us, we were placed under guard by the law. We were kept in protective custody, so to speak, until the way of faith was

revealed. [24] Let me put it another way. The **[Old Testament]** law was our guardian until Christ came; it protected us until we could be made right with God through faith. [25] And now that the way of faith has come, we no longer need the law as our guardian. [26] For you are all children of God through faith in Christ Jesus (Galatians 3:21–26).

To summarize, the Bible not only tells us it is wrong to steal, to lie, to kill, or to be immoral. It also tells us how to get the power we need to help us overcome sin. It shows us how to serve God and how to please God.

The Bible Gives Answers

People are looking for answers today. You can see this in the multitude of conspiracy theories that float on the Internet and surface periodically in the mainstream media. Questions abound for which many people have no easy answers.

- Where did we come from?
- Where are we going?
- What is the meaning of life?
- Was man primitive or advanced in ancient times?
- Is the universe real, or is it just a simulation running on a giant computer?

- Was the world visited by aliens millennia ago?
- Is the world flat?
- Were the moon landings faked by NASA?

You can add others, I'm sure. The fact that highly educated people are taking questions like this seriously shows how badly humans want answers. Some of these people are turning to the Bible in their quest.

The Bible has answers for us. It will not specifically answer all the above questions, but if we accept the answers it does give us, we will have a framework of truth from which to answer all the questions of life we may have in the future.

3

An Overview of the Bible

Organization

We normally divide the Bible into two parts called the Old Testament and the New Testament. Each of these is further divided into sections. We are going to look at these sections in more detail in this book.

The Bible is organized differently from most modern writings. It is a compilation of writings by a large variety of authors. Tim Chaffey states the following:

> The Bible was written over a period of roughly 2,000 years by forty different authors from three continents,

who wrote in three different languages. These facts alone make the Bible one of a kind, but there are many more amazing details that defy natural explanation.

Shepherds, kings, scholars, fishermen, prophets, a military general, a cupbearer, and a priest all penned portions of Scripture. They had different immediate purposes for writing, whether recording history, giving spiritual and moral instruction, or pronouncing judgment. They composed their works from palaces, prisons, the wilderness, and places of exile while writing history, laws, poetry, prophecy, and proverbs. In the process they laid bare their personal emotions, expressing anger, frustration, joy, and love.[1]

Most of the sixty-six books of the Bible are divided into chapters, and the chapters are divided into verses. The chapters do not necessarily denote an outline. Nor do the verses number paragraphs. They are there to make it easier to find passages and quotes. Chapters and verses were added to the Bible over a thousand years after the last books were written.

Written in the East

It is important to remember that the Bible was written in the Eastern Hemisphere, mostly in the area known as the Middle

---

[1] Tim Chaffey, answersingenesis.org, 2011.

East. It reflects Eastern thinking. Scholars and writers from the East, especially during the times the Bible was written, thought and wrote differently than Americans and Europeans do today. Misunderstanding this has led a lot of people to accuse the Bible of contradicting itself.

Here are a few ways Eastern literature differs from today's Western literature.

- Eastern writers exaggerated where we would use an adjective or adverb. (Compare Luke 14:26 with Matthew 10:37.)

- Statements that seem contradictory were viewed as complementing or supplementing each other. (Compare Matthew 27:37, Luke 23:38 and John 19:19.)

- They wrote more by feeling or impression than by outline. (See Ecclesiastes and Revelation.)

- They rounded off numbers. For instance, one writer might talk of 400 years, and another would call it 430 years. (Compare Genesis 15:13, Exodus 12:40, Acts 7:6, Galatians 3:16–17.)

A lot of this doesn't fit our twenty-first century Western compulsion for accuracy, but it was considered normal for readers and writers at the time of Christ and earlier.[2]

---

[2] God used the personalities and cultures of the various writers to express Himself in the Bible.

Names of God's People and Their Land

The Old Testament includes the history of God's people from Creation until about 400 years before the birth of Christ. This allows us to trace the family line of Christ from Adam. The name of God's people varied throughout history. At first, they were generally known as Hebrews. Once they became a nation, they were called Israelites. Since about the fifth century B.C., they have been known as Jews.

The homeland of God's people had a similar shift in names. When Abraham first arrived, the "Promised Land" was known as the land of Canaan. When the Israelites entered Canaan and settled there after their sojourn in Egypt, it became known as the land of Israel. Later, after the nation divided under Rehoboam, the northern part of the land of Israel became known as the Northern Kingdom or Samaria, after its capital city. The southern part was known as the Southern Kingdom or the land of Judah, after the chief tribe living there. Eventually this became Judea. After all the shake-ups under Babylon, Persia, Greece, and Rome, the Promised Land was divided into three main entities: Galilee, Samaria, and Judea. The Roman province of Iudaea included these three areas as well as several beyond the traditional land of Israel.[3]

---

[3] Map by Wikipedia User: Andrew c, CC BY 3.0, https://commons.wikimedia.org/w/index.php?curid=743768

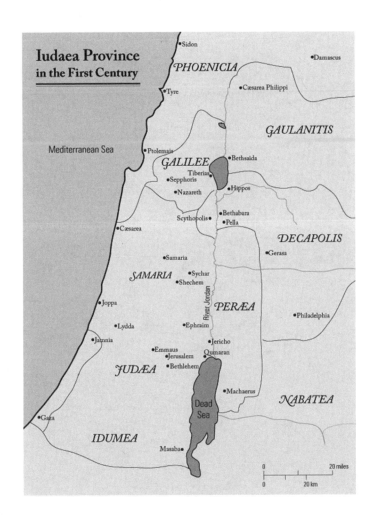

Iudaea Province in the First Century

- Sidon
- Damascus
PHOENICIA
- Tyre
- Cæsarea Philippi

GAULANITIS

Mediterranean Sea
- Ptolemais
GALILEE
- Bethsaida
Tiberias
- Sepphoris
- Nazareth
- Hippos

- Bethabara
Scythopolis
- Pella
- Cæsarea

DECAPOLIS
- Gerasa

- Samaria
SAMARIA
- Sychar
- Shechem

- Joppa
PERÆA
- Philadelphia

- Lydda
- Ephraim
- Jamnia
- Jericho
- Emmaus
- Qumaran
- Jerusalem
- Bethlehem
JUDÆA

NABATEA
- Machaerus

Dead
Sea
- Gaza
IDUMEA
Masaba

River Jordan

0 — 20 miles
0 — 20 km

4

The Old Testament

We are going to skim through the whole Bible in the next few chapters. We have listed these books in the order you will find them in the Bible. If you are using this book as a reading guide to the Bible, you should consider jumping ahead to the New Testament and starting with the Gospel of Matthew.

If you are using this guide simply to become more familiar with the books of the Bible, continue from here.

Books by Moses (the Pentateuch)

Moses was a great prophet of God. He wrote approximately 20 percent of the Bible, about the same amount Paul later wrote.

Moses' parents were Hebrew slaves in Egypt during a time when Pharaoh had ordered that all Hebrew baby boys were to be drowned at birth. Moses' mother hid him among the weeds along the river, where Pharaoh's daughter found him. His own mother was hired to nurse and care for him as a small child. Eventually Moses was taken to Egypt and raised in Pharaoh's palace. According to ancient historians like Josephus, he was the general of Egypt's army and a possible heir to the throne. But at the age of forty, he ran afoul of Egyptian law and had to flee for his life.

Moses lived in the desert for the next forty years, where he married and raised a family. But later, when he was about eighty years old, God called him back to Egypt to deliver the Hebrews from their bondage. He was to take them back to Canaan, where their forefathers, Abraham, Isaac, and Jacob, had lived.

Moses wrote or compiled the first five books of the Old Testament during the forty years he led the Hebrews in the desert of Sinai. I will list the books here, with a summary of each.

Genesis

The Bible's first book starts at the beginning. It gives the story of Creation and the Fall of mankind into sin. It continues with the story of how the people on earth grew increasingly wicked. They finally filled the earth with violence, and God decided to destroy all living people except Noah and his family. Genesis tells how Noah built the ark and God destroyed humanity by flooding the whole world.

Noah's family started to repopulate the earth after the Flood, but sin overtook them again. God scattered the earth's inhabitants at the Tower of Babel by confusing their languages. This kept sin from ruling the earth again as it had before the Flood.[1]

All of this is recorded in the first eleven chapters. This first section of Genesis also includes three long lists of genealogies which will not mean much to the beginning reader. You can safely scan through them or even skip them for now.

In Chapter 12, we finally get to Abraham, the main character of Genesis. His story takes the next thirteen chapters—a quarter of Genesis. Then come the stories of Isaac, Jacob, and Joseph, Abraham's descendants. Joseph's story, especially, is a favorite of many. Most of these characters' lives overlapped with each other, even though it doesn't seem that way in Genesis. According to the chronology given in Genesis, Noah probably didn't die until around the time Abraham was born. Jacob was around fifteen years old when Abraham died.

The book of Genesis covers close to 2,500 years of history and ends with Jacob's family moving to Egypt to survive a famine.

Exodus

Exodus begins with the story of Moses. It covers the first

---

[1] This didn't keep people from sinning, but it kept sin from becoming a powerful, politically unified force as it was before the Flood.

eighty years of his life in the first four chapters before coming to the main story of this book. Between the end of Genesis and the beginning of Exodus, God's people had grown from a family of about seventy people to a small nation. When they left Egypt with Moses, they numbered about 600,000 men, plus women and children. This suggests a group of at least 2.5 million people.

Exodus includes the story of the ten plagues which crippled Egypt to the point that Pharaoh ordered the enslaved Hebrews to leave. Chapters 13 to 15 tell the story of their leaving and crossing the Red Sea. Chapters 16 to 19 talk about the group's experiences in the desert.

The rest of the book has the first listing of the Old Testament laws, starting with the Ten Commandments.[2] If this is your first time reading the Old Testament, you may want to scan most of the last part of the book except for the accounts in Chapter 24 and Chapters 32 to 34. I'm not suggesting that the list of laws and the instructions for building the tabernacle aren't important. But if you are simply trying to get a feel for the story of God's people, you can come back to that later when you are interested in more details.

---

[2] See Exodus 20:1–21.

Leviticus

Most of the book of Leviticus consists of more laws and procedures for worshipping God. It describes the beginning of the Jewish priesthood in Chapters 8 to 10. Chapters 11 to 15 have instructions about food they were not to eat, and it describes health procedures for avoiding infectious diseases. If this is your first reading of the Old Testament, you will probably either skip Leviticus or briefly scan it.

Numbers

The Israelites spent their first year of freedom in the Sinai Desert, building the tabernacle and learning how to put into practice the laws God gave to Moses during that time. The first ten chapters of Numbers cover the preparations to leave Sinai and travel to the Promised Land. Chapter 1 contains a census, and Chapter 2 describes the arrangement of the camp. Chapters 3 and 4 list the duties of the Levites and Kohathites. Among other things, Chapter 5 describes an interesting test used to find out if a wife had committed adultery. Chapters 6 to 10 tell about preparing for the first Passover. Finally, in Chapter 10, the Israelites started their journey to the Promised Land.

Things didn't go well for them. When they left Egypt, a lot

of Egyptian rabble came with them.[3] It appears that before long, these people started to wish they had stayed in Egypt. Their discontent quickly rubbed off on the Israelites. Chapter 11 describes the first trouble between the Israelites and God. In Chapter 12, Aaron and Miriam, Moses' brother and sister, rebelled against his leadership. God punished them by striking Miriam with leprosy. God healed her when Moses prayed for her, but she had to be separated from the group. She spent seven days outside the camp while the Israelites waited for her.

Finally, despite these troubles, the Israelites got close to the Promised Land, as shown in the last verse of Chapter 12. In Chapter 13, they sent twelve spies to explore it. The land was exceptionally fertile, but the inhabitants were big and strong. Except for two men called Joshua and Caleb, the spies brought back a bad report. They said they felt like grasshoppers beside the people in Canaan and would never be able to conquer the land. Chapter 13 tells about their fear and the massive backlash of the people against Moses for bringing them into this situation. God brought it back under control by opening the ground and swallowing up the leaders of the rebellion. God then forbade anyone who was twenty-one years old or older at that time to ever enter Canaan. As a result, the Israelites spent the

---

[3] The Bible calls them a "mixed multitude." They set up their tents around the edge of the camp when the Israelites stopped, rather than being given specific places within the camp. This would indicate they weren't Israelites.

next thirty-eight years in the desert.[4]

The book skips most of the next thirty-five years or so, then records some interesting incidents in the latter part of their stay in the desert. Moses got angry at the people, and God wouldn't let him enter the Promised Land. A witch doctor named Balaam was scolded by his donkey when he tried to curse the Israelites. Instead of cursing them, he blessed them. But then without much hesitation, he turned around and told their enemies how to destroy them through immorality. Finally, in Chapter 26, the Israelites took another census, and not a person remained among them (except Joshua and Caleb) who had been counted in Sinai years before.

The rest of the book describes more directives, another war, and instructions on dividing the land of Canaan once they had conquered it.

Deuteronomy

This book is the longest sermon recorded in the Bible. In it, Moses reviewed the entire forty years since they had left Egypt. He recounted their victories and their defeats. He reiterated the Ten Commandments and many of the other laws given in earlier books.

He also warned the Israelites, reminding them that the

---

[4] They spent a total of forty years in the desert from the time they left Egypt until they entered Canaan, but two of those years were spent getting to Canaan the first time.

Canaanites were losing their land because of their wicked-ness. God's people would also lose it if they became wicked.

These five books are a great monument to a mighty leader. They are the foundation for the rest of the Bible. They are quoted from or alluded to hundreds of times by other prophets, by Jesus, and by the apostles who wrote the New Testament.[5]

Books of History

This section of the Bible has twelve books. They cover about a thousand years of history. They overlap in some cases, but each book gives extra details and a different perspective.

Joshua, the first book in this section, continues the story of the Israelites after Moses' death. During this time, the Israelites conquered Canaan and divided it among their twelve tribes. Two and a half tribes stayed on the east side of the Jordan River, but the rest settled in Canaan. For almost four hundred years, they were ruled by judges. Then they asked God to give them a king. Four kings later, the ten northern tribes broke away from the rest of Israel. They repeatedly rebelled against God, and eventually the king of Assyria defeated them. The Assyrians deported them, scattering them throughout various nations where they were gradually assimilated into the local

---

[5] There are over 120 direct quotations in the New Testament.

culture. The main exception to this was the group known as the Samaritans. These people were the descendants of a small group of Jews who intermarried with the inhabitants of other conquered lands.[6]

A century or so later, the Southern Kingdom was overthrown by Babylon, and most of the inhabitants were taken to Babylon as slaves. Seventy year later, the king of the Medes and Persians released them to return to their homeland. The story ends with a Jewish girl being crowned queen of Persia and saving her people from being wiped out by the regent of Persia.

It is an exciting story, especially if you enjoy history. A lot can happen in a thousand years.

Joshua

Joshua was one of the twelve spies. He was Moses' servant during the time the Israelites spent in the desert, and he acted as the general of Israel's army. God then chose him to replace Moses as leader of the Israelites.

This book tells the story of the invasion of Canaan, starting with Jericho. The war lasted around seven years, after which

---

[6] The Assyrians had a policy of disbursing conquered peoples among other nations they had conquered. They left a small number of Jews in Samaria and deported the rest, scattering them among other nations. They then did the same to other nations, deporting them and placing some of them in Samaria. This resulted in the Samaritans' mixed bloodline that was despised by genuine Jews.

they divided the land among the tribes. The armies of Israel had wiped out the main resistance, but many of the tribes continued to face local opposition from the Canaanites. They eventually made peace with these people rather than driving them out as God had commanded.

The first eleven chapters of Joshua describe the invasion and conquest of Canaan. Chapters 12 to 22 tell about the division of the land after the war. Like Moses, Joshua gathered the Israelites together before he died. His parting discourse starts in Chapter 23, and he challenged the people to make the choice to serve God. Unfortunately, many of his fears for Israel came true in later years.

Judges

It is difficult to construct a timeline of the book of Judges. Some of the judges overlapped with each other and ruled in various parts of the country.

God had warned the Israelites not to allow any Canaanites to stay in the land after they settled there. However, the Israelites were tired of war and didn't follow God's commands. Because of this, God told them (in Judges 2:1–5) He would allow the Canaanites to be a snare to them. The book of Judges describes this process. Over and over, the Israelites sinned, and God used the people of the land to punish them. Finally, in desperation, they would cry out to

God, and He would raise up a judge to deliver them. But their allegiance to God never lasted very long.

The last verse in Judges summarizes the whole book very well. "In those days there was no king in Israel; everyone did what was right in his own eyes" (Judges 21:25).

Ruth

This book is refreshing to read after the chaos of Judges. It is a simple story of a family who moved from Israel to the neighboring country of Moab during a famine. While living there, the two sons married Moabite girls. Then the father and the two sons died. Naomi, the mother, and Ruth, her Moabite daughter-in-law, returned to Israel completely destitute.

To understand the rest of the story, you need to know about the ancient practice of Levirate marriage. This practice has existed (and still does) in various cultures throughout the world. God introduced the Jewish version of it in Deuteronomy 25:5–6. In short, if a man died childless, his oldest brother was to marry his widow, even if he already had a wife and family. Any children born to the widow would inherit the belongings of the dead man. It was a way to keep a family line from dying out among the Israelites. It was also a way to support a destitute widow.

In the book of Ruth, this happened with a double twist. Naomi didn't marry again, but one of Naomi's close relatives married Naomi's heiress, her daughter-in-law, Ruth.

1 Samuel

Samuel was the last of Israel's judges. This book begins with the birth of Samuel as a direct answer to his mother's prayer for a son. His mother lent him to God as she had promised she would, and he went to live at the temple. Eli, the high priest and judge of that time, raised young Samuel.

The story of Samuel's calling is very interesting. He was sleeping one night when a voice called him. Thinking Eli wanted him, he ran to the old man. But Eli hadn't called him. This happened several times before Eli realized that God was calling the child. He instructed Samuel in the proper way to answer God, and God gave Samuel his first message. It predicted the death of Eli because he hadn't obeyed God in restraining his wicked sons.

The book goes on to tell of Samuel's life as a judge in Israel. But his sons didn't turn out much better than Eli's had, so the people came to Samuel and asked for a king. Samuel interpreted this as a rejection of God and warned them against it. But at their insistence, God told him to go ahead and crown Saul as the first king of Israel (see Chapter 9). Saul ruled for forty years, but eventually drifted away from God. Chapter 15 tells how God finally rejected Saul as king, and in Chapter 17, Samuel anointed young David to succeed Saul.

The rest of the book recounts the story of David before he was crowned king. In Chapter 17, we have the famous story of David defeating the giant Goliath. In Chapters 18 and 19, Saul's jealousy of David boiled over, and he tried to kill David. However, David escaped and became the leader of a disgruntled band. Samuel died in Chapter 25, and Saul fell in battle in Chapter 31 after having tried to contact Samuel's spirit through a witch.

2 Samuel

The second book of Samuel provides us with an account of the forty years David reigned as king. It begins with his coronation and ends with his death.

This book takes an honest look at both the good and bad points of a man who served God. David was devoted to God, but even so, he failed at times. For instance, he had an affair with the wife of one of his soldiers, then had her husband killed to cover up the fact. God sent a prophet to rebuke him, and David admitted his sin. He wrote Psalm 51 as an expression of his genuine repentance.

David had a lot of trouble in his household as a result of his sin. One of David's sons raped his half sister. Her brother then killed the rapist. This brother then tried to take over David's kingdom, and David's general killed the young man. Clearly, the Bible doesn't hide the dark side of even its greatest heroes. However, the New Testament calls David a man after God's own heart. If you are a person who is struggling with sin, the story of David should give you hope.

1 Kings

The book of 1 Kings continues the story where 2 Samuel left off. David's son, Solomon, ascended to the throne at the age of twenty. The first eleven chapters give his life story and tell us about his wisdom and wealth. During this period, Israel reached the zenith of its greatness. This was also the only time in Israel's history that its land base reached what God had originally intended them to have.

Solomon got off to a good start in his reign. He pleased God, and God promised him wisdom, long life, and great riches. Solomon built a temple for God, to replace the tabernacle Israel was still using. He wrote 3,000 proverbs and 1,005 songs. One of these songs was the Song of Solomon, and the book of Proverbs preserves many of his wise sayings.

"But King Solomon loved many strange women." That is how 1 Kings 11:1 (in the King James Version) introduces the downfall of Solomon. This chapter goes on to tell the story of his capitulation to the false gods his wives worshipped.

From here, the pace speeds up. The ten northern tribes rebelled against Solomon's son Rehoboam, dividing the kingdom. King followed king in both the Northern Kingdom and the Southern Kingdom. Some kings were godly, but the majority were not, especially the northern kings. They worshipped idols and caused their people to sin.

In Chapter 17, Elijah appeared in the Northern Kingdom. He was one of the greatest prophets, and much of the rest of 1 Kings tells of him and his work. In Chapter 19, he called Elisha to be his helper.

2 Kings

This book begins (in Chapter 2) with a fiery chariot and horses taking Elijah to heaven in a whirlwind. Elijah threw his mantle from the chariot as he departed, leaving it for Elisha as a badge of office. Elisha succeeded him in a ministry that lasted about fifty years.

Some of the highlights of the book are:

- Elijah is taken to heaven in a fiery chariot and horses (Chapter 2)
- Elisha performs four miracles (Chapter 4)
- A Syrian captain is healed of leprosy (Chapter 5)
- An axe head floats on water (Chapter 6)
- Jehu seizes control of the Northern Kingdom (Chapters 9 and 10)
- Elisha dies (Chapter 13)

- Fall of the Northern Kingdom (Chapter 17)
- Sennacherib attacks Judah (Chapters 18 and 19)
- King Josiah restores the temple and worship of God (Chapters 22 and 23)
- The Southern Kingdom falls, and Judah goes into exile (Chapters 24 and 25)

This book covers well over a century of Israel's history. It shows us the final fulfillment of the warnings Moses and Joshua had given to the Israelites. It also ends on a dark note with the Israelites in exile.

1 Chronicles

First and 2 Chronicles go over the same basic territory covered by 1 and 2 Kings. They condense some parts of the history, but add details to others. First Chronicles covers David's reign, but places more emphasis on his preparations for worship and less on his faults and wars than 1 Kings does.

Ezra is thought to have compiled these two books to place the Israelites on a proper foundation after they returned to their homeland. Genealogy was important to the Jewish religious system, so 1 Chronicles starts off with ten chapters of genealogy. Other shorter listings are interspersed throughout the two books. This allowed them to confirm the credentials of the priests and Levites. While these lists may be interesting to a few Bible scholars, the rest of us will normally skip them or just scan through them.

2 Chronicles

Second Chronicles starts with Solomon's reign and covers the same period of history as 2 Kings does. However, it concentrates on the Southern Kingdom and the lineage of David. Since this book was compiled after the Jewish captivity, it adds a note at the end about the Jews returning to their homeland. This leaves us with an optimistic view of the future.

Ezra

The book of Ezra starts where 2 Chronicles left off, and it tells about the restoration of the Jews to their homeland (now called Judah). It records the journey of several large expeditions of Jews from Babylon to Jerusalem. Zerubbabel led the first group, and Ezra led the second one about a generation later.

The king of Persia commissioned Ezra to teach the people how to serve God, and Ezra took this task seriously. He discovered that the Jews who had returned earlier had already drifted away from following the laws of Moses. Many had intermarried with the people of the land around them. Ezra led a great revival that put an end to much of this sin. Ezra's actions might seem harsh to us, but he is probably to be credited that the Jews did not entirely lose their identity.

Nehemiah

The book of Nehemiah was part of Ezra at one point, and the same person probably wrote both. The first group of Jews to return to Judah had rebuilt the temple, but the walls of Jerusalem had not been repaired. This allowed robbers and the rabble of the land to encroach on the people living there. Nehemiah's first concern was to rebuild the wall.

His second concern was the same as the one expressed in Ezra. The last half of Nehemiah tells about the revival led by Ezra and the repercussions of it.

Both Nehemiah and Ezra were passionate about bringing revival to the nation of Israel.

Esther

This is the last book in the historical section of the Old Testament. Like Ruth, it tells the story of a woman who played a vital role in the history of God's people.

The Persian kings were suffering military defeats, and Persia's greatness was waning during this time. The book doesn't mention this, but knowing it helps us understand the setting.

Esther was a Jewish orphan raised by her older cousin. The queen of Persia embarrassed the king by refusing to obey a direct order he had given her in front of a large group of important people. In his fury, the king dismissed her and went looking for another queen to take her place. At the end of a year's searching, the king chose Esther from a large group of beautiful young women.

The book also includes the story of how Esther defeated the plans of Haman (the vice-regent of Persia) to wipe out all the Jews in Persia.

This is the only book in the Bible that never mentions God directly.

Poetry and Wisdom

This section consists of five books. These books are not interwoven or dependent on each other like the books in the last two sections were. Each book has its own topic and its own way of approaching the topic. Even the structure of the books varies from one to the other.

All five of these books are poetic in form. But in ancient times, that didn't mean the lines rhymed. Poetic form was used for effect, to cause emotion, and to aid in memorization. Most of the oldest literary records archeologists have found were written in poetic form.

These books are also part of what is called wisdom literature. According to one source, wisdom literature is defined as literature that "consists of statements by sages and wise men that offer teachings about divinity and virtue."[7] The five books we are looking

---

[7] https://en.wikipedia.org/wiki/Wisdom_literature

at here are among the most famous examples of ancient wisdom literature. In the Septuagint Greek translation of the Hebrew Bible, two more books were added, the Book of Wisdom and Sirach.

Job

The theme of the book of Job is the age-old question, "Why do bad things happen to good people?" You may find the discussion tedious, but you should at least read the first two chapters and the last five.

Job was the richest man in his country and is thought to have lived even before the time of Abraham. He was a devout follower of God.

One day God talked about Job and his good character in a conversation with Satan. Satan challenged God to give him a chance to turn Job away from Him. He claimed that Job only served God because of the benefits he got from it, and that if things went wrong for Job, he would curse God. God did not agree, so He gave Satan permission to destroy Job's family and all his wealth. All he had left after this was several servants and his wife.

Job grieved deeply, but he refused to curse God. Satan came back to talk to God again and told Him that if he could touch Job's body, Job would curse God. God gave him permission to touch Job but not to take his life. Satan struck Job with painful boils all over his body, but Job still refused to curse God.

This all took place in the first several chapters. The main part of the book is a dialog between Job and three friends who came to comfort him in his distress. Job was so miserable that his friends just sat there with him for a whole week with no one saying a word. Finally, Job started to talk about his misery, expecting his friends to sympathize with him.

His friends, however, presented a different opinion. They were convinced God had sent Job's calamities as a punishment for some sin he had committed. Job disagreed vehemently. The dialog went around and around this theme with both sides becoming increasingly adamant.

In Chapter 38, God finally spoke up. Most of the rest of the book is this final dialog between God and Job. God never answered Job's question about why bad things happened to good people. But Job realized that God was so great that He didn't need to answer. Job could trust God even if he didn't understand.

Psalms

The book of Psalms is a collection of 150 psalms, many written by King David.[8] Think of it as a poetry book or a songbook. Many people have used the psalms as songs through the years.

---

[8] Each psalm should be referred to as a psalm, not a chapter. For instance, we refer to Psalm 23 or the 23rd Psalm, not Psalms chapter 23 or the 23rd chapter of Psalms.

Bible students often divide the book of Psalms into five sections. These sections do not have a central theme, because the subject matter can vary widely from psalm to psalm. Some are poems of praise. Some express depression or even anger. A few psalms, such as Psalm 137, show human feelings at their worst. And some, like Psalm 51, are expressions of repentance.[9]

The poetic form of the psalms is not as easy to see in English as it was in Hebrew.[10] But even in English, you can see the parallelism of thought and word usage typical of Hebrew poetry. Rather than using words that sounded alike, they used ideas that sounded alike.

You will discover some psalms you really like and some that don't mean as much to you. A survey revealed that these are the favorite ten psalms in order of preference: Psalm 23, 121, 138, 62, 46, 117, 37, 1, 40, 84.[11]

---

[9] "What must be said . . . is that the Psalms are poems, and poems intended to be sung: not doctrinal treatises, nor even sermons. . . . Most emphatically the Psalms must be read as poems; as lyrics, with all the licenses and all the formalities, the hyperboles, the emotional rather than logical connections, which are proper to lyric poetry. They must be read as poems if they are to be understood; no less than French must be read as French or English as English. Otherwise we shall miss what is in them and think we see what is not." — As quoted by Ronald Barclay Allen, *Praise! A Matter of Life and Breath* (Nashville: Thomas Nelson Publishers, 1980), pp. 23–24.

[10] See the following website for more detail: https://bible.org/seriespage/2-what-psalm

[11] http://www.biblesummary.info/blog/2012/04/top-10-psalms

Proverbs

The book of Proverbs is a compilation of wise sayings. Solomon wrote much of the book, but not all of it. He may have compiled some parts of it from other sources. Also, later editors added more of Solomon's proverbs (see Proverbs 25—29) and proverbs by other authors (Proverbs 30—31). We can outline the book as follows:

- Proverbs 1–9: Proverbs of Solomon, Son of David, King of Israel
- Proverbs 10–22:16: Proverbs of Solomon
- Proverbs 22:17–24:34: The Sayings of the Wise[12]
- Proverbs 25–29: Proverbs of Solomon That the Officials of King Hezekiah of Judah Copied
- Proverbs 30: The Words of Agur
- Proverbs 31:1–9: The Words of King Lemuel of Massa, Which His Mother Taught Him
- Proverbs 31:10–31: The Ideal Wise Woman (elsewhere called The Woman of Substance).[13]

Solomon, unfortunately, failed many of the tests he gave

---

[12] Most translations divide this section into two, "The Sayings of the Wise" and "More Sayings of the Wise."

[13] This outline is taken from the book *Proverbs: A Bible Commentary for Teaching and Preaching* by Leo G. Perdue (Louisville, KY: Westminster John Knox Press, 2012).

in Proverbs. The theme of the book seems to be "the fear of the Lord is the beginning of wisdom." It includes many good thoughts and observations, warnings against immoral conduct, and wise sayings. The first nine chapters contain longer passages that tie together, but after that, most of the proverbs are concise, independent maxims.

Ecclesiastes

The book of Ecclesiastes gives the philosophical backing for the book of Job. The questions Solomon faced are like the questions faced by Job, though the two scenarios vary widely.

In Ecclesiastes, Solomon pictured himself as a wise sage trying to penetrate the secrets of existence. He believed life must have more meaning than he saw on the surface. Everywhere he looked, he saw vanity. He pictured the universe as a giant perpetual motion machine. Someone created it, turned on the switch, and let it run on its own. For people caught within this meaningless system, death was the only way out. If something went wrong, the whole machine would self-destruct.

Solomon kept shifting his focus as he wrote. At first, he was a skeptic. Later, he was a philosopher. Gradually, he brought God into the picture. But he kept bouncing back and forth between believing that Fate or God controlled the universe.

Eastern thought process comes through very clearly in this book. Solomon seems to contradict himself as he shifts his focus from one spot to the other. It is best not to decide what he was really after until you have read the whole book several times.

He does finally reach a conclusion in the last chapter: "Fear God and keep his commandments, for this is the whole duty of man" (12:13, KJV). After all the effort expended in writing the book, this seems anticlimactic. But Solomon wrote this book mostly from a secular perspective. This could have been because of his spiritual condition in his later years, or it could have been a deliberate literary device. With only a few exceptions, he used data he gathered with his five senses to support his ideas. He didn't speak of eternity, and his conception of God was bland and distant.

Song of Solomon

This book is one long poem written by Solomon. He seems to have written it for public reading, perhaps at one of his own weddings. It is a dialog between a prospective bride and bridegroom, with the "daughters of Jerusalem" acting as a chorus to fill in the gaps.

Some rabbis disapproved of the Song of Solomon and taught that no one under age thirty should read it. Most rabbis interpreted it as an allegory of the love between God and Israel. Christian teachers sometimes use it as an allegory of Christ and the Church.

Probably the Song of Solomon is what it seems to be—a poem written to commemorate the joys of human love.

Major Prophets

A prophet is a person who speaks for God. While some prophecies foretell the future, that is not the Bible prophet's primary job description. Much of Old Testament prophecy was centered around warning people of the consequences if they did not change their ways. It was not a concrete foretelling of the future. Rather, it foretold what would happen IF people did not change their ways. As one writer says, "The thrust of God's prophecies is to encourage good human behavior. Human behavior—not forces beyond human control—determines whether the future will be bright or dismal."[14]

Old Testament prophecies about the coming Messiah were more concrete. But even they were often couched in figurative language which made them easier to interpret after the fact than before.

This section of the Old Testament begins with five books considered to be the Major Prophets. These books are mostly longer than the twelve books that follow them, called the Minor Prophets. Note that the terms major and minor do not refer to the importance of the prophet, but to the amount of writing he did.

Historically, the Major Prophets are in chronological order, starting well before the exile of the Southern Kingdom. The

---

[14] Michael Gantt, *NonChurchgoer's Guide to the Bible,* Good Books, Intercourse, PA, 1995, p. 116.

Minor Prophets overlap the Major Prophets. For instance, Hosea was a contemporary of Isaiah.

Isaiah

The book of Isaiah is sometimes called the Gospel of the Old Testament. Isaiah represents New Testament values more clearly than any other Old Testament book.

The book can be divided several ways. The first thirty-three chapters speak of a coming judgment (the exile to Babylon) and its repercussions. The rest of the book speaks of the restoration of Israel after the exile. Passages about the coming Messiah, such as Isaiah 40, are interwoven throughout the book.

Some of the best examples of Bible literature are found in this book. The New Testament quotes Isaiah more often than any other Old Testament book.

Jeremiah

Jeremiah lived through the fall of Jerusalem, and that is reflected in his writing. In fact, the book includes various sections describing the last days of the Southern Kingdom.

Jeremiah also prophesied about the destruction of Babylon and several other nations in the same general area. This book is one of the more personal ones in the Old Testament. Jeremiah's message was often rejected, and the book shows his emotional reactions more clearly than most Biblical writings do.

Lamentations

Tradition points to Jeremiah as the author of this book as well. It records the emotion he felt while watching the destruction of Jerusalem and the slaughter of its people. The prophet had a genuine love and compassion for his people even though he understood the reasons for their judgment.

Despite the sorrow and turmoil in Jeremiah's heart, he still had hope for the future.

This book is a poem about the same length as the Song of Solomon.

Ezekiel

Ezekiel was a prophet living among the exiled Jews in Babylon (the empire, not the city). He prophesied for over twenty years.

Ezekiel's message is one of judgment and restoration. The first thirty-two chapters focus on sin and judgment, speaking both to the exiled Jews and the surrounding nations. The rest of the book tells about the restoration of God's people and looks ahead to the Messiah and His coming kingdom.

This book is one of more difficult ones in the Bible. It contains a lot of figurative and apocalyptic language, especially in the latter part of the book.

Daniel

Like Ezekiel, Daniel was taken captive during the invasions of Judea. The first six chapters of this book describe his life in Babylon and include well-known accounts such as the deliverance from the fiery furnace and Daniel in the lion's den. The latter part of the book speaks of the restoration of God's kingdom and the coming of the Messiah. Daniel strongly emphasizes the sovereignty of God over the affairs of men.

Minor Prophets

Hosea

We know very little of this prophet's background except what he tells us in his book. Besides his writing, God used him as an object lesson to Israel. He married a prostitute who bore him three children. She was unfaithful to him, but he bought her back out of slavery. This depicts in real life Israel's relationship with God.

Joel

The theme of this book is the Day of the Lord—a period of judgment and restoration for God's people. It is often interpreted as being apocalyptic in nature and speaking of the final Day of the Lord.

Amos

The prophet Amos was a shepherd and gatherer of sycamore fruit. He came from the Southern Kingdom, but his prophecies were aimed at the Northern Kingdom and surrounding nations. Jeroboam II reigned over the Northern Kingdom at that time. It was a prosperous time, and the rich took advantage of the poor. Amos preached a strong message of justice and mercy, proclaiming God's judgment on arrogant materialism.

Obadiah

This is the shortest book in the Old Testament. Like Joel, its theme is the Day of the Lord. It is also an indictment against Edom for taking advantage of the plight of those who fled from Jerusalem when it was invaded.

Jonah

Jonah was from the Northern Kingdom, and his message was to be delivered to Assyria, Israel's greatest enemy at the time. He rebelled against preaching in Syria's capital, Nineveh, and ran away in the opposite direction. God used a storm and a big fish to get him back on track, and he finally went to Assyria. His message was successful, and a revival swept over Nineveh, with even the king repenting in sackcloth and ashes. Rather than rejoicing, Jonah was upset. God rebuked him for this, and the book abruptly ends on that note.

Micah

Micah aimed his message toward Samaria and Jerusalem. Along with warnings of judgment, he foretold the birth of Jesus in Bethlehem. He also gave a vivid picture of the kingdom of God under the reign of the Messiah. Samaria fell to the Assyrians during his time as a prophet, vindicating what he had said.

Nahum

Nahum is thought to have prophesied during the reign of King Manasseh. This was possibly the lowest period in Judah's history, with the nation having turned almost completely away from God to idols. The bulk of the book is focused on the coming judgment of Nineveh nearly a century after the revival there under Jonah's prophecy.

Habakkuk

Habakkuk asks an interesting question: Why would God use a wicked nation like Babylon to punish His people? The book records a dialog between the prophet and God. God told Habakkuk that the just shall live by faith. In other words, trust God. He will set all things right in His own time.

Zephaniah

Zephaniah was the great-great grandson of King Hezekiah. This probably made him a distant cousin of King Josiah, the king who reigned during his prophecy. The book follows the familiar pattern of foretelling judgment and then restoration. Zephaniah quotes from the Law frequently. This is interesting because according to 2 Chronicles 34:8–33, all copies of the Law of Moses had been lost before Josiah's reign. One copy was found hidden in the temple and spurred a revival in Judah. Apparently, Zephaniah had access to a copy of these scrolls.

Haggai

Haggai wrote his book to encourage the rebuilding of the temple. The Jews had been back in the Promised Land about eighteen years but had not finished rebuilding the temple. It seems Haggai had seen the original temple before its destruction by the Babylonians. This means he would have been over seventy years old at the time he wrote this book. The people listened to his words and rebuilt the temple.

Zechariah

Haggai and Zechariah are both mentioned in the book of Ezra, and the two were contemporaries. Zechariah was much younger, however. The first part of the book addresses the Jews who were struggling to rebuild the temple. The latter part was probably written much later, before Ezra and Nehemiah arrived in Jerusalem.

Malachi

This book gives us the last glimpse of God's people before the New Testament era. It probably overlaps with the latter part of Nehemiah, because Malachi's concerns are similar to Nehemiah's. The Israelites had been back in the Promised Land for a century or so, and spiritual apathy had penetrated to the very heart of the land.

The Messiah was coming, but first the Jews faced 400 years of silence. No more revelations, no more prophets, but then—the Messiah!

5

The New Testament

If you are new to the Bible, the New Testament will introduce you to the most important character of the Bible, Jesus Christ. Even though many Jews didn't accept Him when He came, Jesus was the Messiah they had been waiting for ever since Malachi wrote the final installment of the Old Testament four hundred years earlier.

The Gospels and Acts

If you are using this book as a reading guide, you should start reading at the Gospel of Matthew. The Gospels tell the story of Jesus from four perspectives by four different writers.

Matthew, Mark, and Luke cover a similar scope. John wrote his gospel later than the others and from a different perspective. To get the complete story, you should read all four of the Gospels. Acts is a sequel to the book of Luke and speaks about the first years of the church.

Matthew

The Jews expected the Messiah to come and set up a kingdom for them. Because of this, excitement swept Jerusalem and Judea when John the Baptist started preaching, "Repent, for the kingdom of heaven is at hand." They were expecting an earthly king who would set up a Jewish kingdom and drive the Romans out of Palestine. As we know, this didn't happen. Jesus came to set up a spiritual kingdom, the kingdom of heaven. Many Jews were disappointed by this. Even Jesus' disciples had a hard time understanding it.

Matthew wrote his gospel to show the Jewish people what God's kingdom is like. It includes over fifty quotations directly from the Old Testament, as well as many indirect quotations. He wanted the Jews to see that Jesus was the Messiah they had been looking for even though He did not set up the earthly kingdom they expected. Matthew even included a lengthy genealogy at the beginning of his gospel, tracing the official ancestry of Jesus back through Joseph to David and Abraham.

This gospel gives a beautiful picture of Jesus as a king. Chapters

4 to 25 cover His teachings and ministry. Chapters 26 and 27 tell of His death, and Chapter 28 recounts His resurrection.

Chapters 5 to 7 contain the Sermon on the Mount, a definitive look at the difference between God's expectations in the Old Testament and the New Testament. It is the longest of Jesus' sermons recorded in the New Testament. These chapters give one of the best summaries found in the Bible of what God expects from His followers.

Theme verse: "*She will bring forth a Son, and you shall call His name JESUS, for He will save His people from their sins*" (Matthew 1:21).

Mark

Mark is the shortest gospel. Mark pictured Jesus as a servant. To do this, he focused especially on what Jesus did. He didn't always write in chronological order, as you will see if you compare his gospel with some of the others.

Mark shows us the compassion of Jesus as well as His authority. This is vividly portrayed by the many miracles Mark recorded.

This gospel is sometimes called Peter's gospel. Mark was closely associated with Peter years after Jesus' resurrection, and he is thought to have summarized Peter's understanding of the life of Jesus.

Theme verse: *"For even the Son of Man did not come to be served, but to serve, and to give His life a ransom for many"* (Mark 10:45).

Luke

Luke was the only Gentile (non-Jewish) writer of a Bible book. He was a doctor and wrote like a true historian from his own research (see Luke 1:3). His gospel is twice the length of Mark's and is the longest book in the New Testament. The Gospel of Luke, like the Gospel of Matthew, contains a genealogy of Jesus, but this one goes all the way back to Adam instead of stopping with Abraham.

Luke approached the story of Jesus from the perspective that Jesus was a man. But Jesus was not just any man—He was the Savior. Luke wrote his account for Theophilus, a Gentile convert who was not necessarily acquainted with the Jews or the life of Christ, so Luke wrote in more detail than the other gospel writers.

Theme verse: *"For the Son of Man has come to seek and to save that which was lost"* (Luke 19:10).

John

John's stated purpose in writing this gospel was to help his readers "believe that Jesus is the Christ, the Son of God, and that believing you may have life in His name" (John 20:31).

He repeated this emphasis on Jesus being the Son of God in various accounts throughout the gospel.

This list of the "I am" statements of Christ clearly shows this focus.

- "I am the bread of life" (John 6:35, 41, 48, 51)
- "I am from [God], and He sent Me" (John 7:29)
- "I am the light of the world" (John 8:12; 9:5)
- "I AM [God]" (John 8:58)
- "I am the door" (John 10:7, 9)
- "I am the good shepherd" (John 10:11, 14)
- "I am the Son of God" (John 10:36)
- "I am the resurrection and the life" (John 11:25)
- "I am the way and the truth and the life" (John 14:6)
- "I am the vine" (John 15:1, 5)

John wrote his gospel from a radically different perspective than the other three. He wrote many years[1] after the other three writers and apparently focused on areas the others didn't include. For instance, he wrote almost six

---

[1] He wrote toward the end of his life, according to Polycarp, a second-century leader who knew John personally. This could have been around thirty years after Peter and Paul were executed and sixty years after Jesus died. John was probably the youngest of the apostles and the only one to die a natural death.

chapters dealing with the last week of Jesus' life.

John also wrote three short epistles and the book of Revelation. We will look at them later.

Theme verses: *In the beginning was the Word, and the Word was with God, and the Word was God . . . And the Word became flesh and dwelt among us, and we beheld His glory, the glory as of the only begotten of the Father, full of grace and truth* (John 1:1, 14).

Acts

The book of Acts continues where the Gospel of Luke left off. Luke must have spent some time with Peter, as well as traveled with Paul. This would explain why the first twelve chapters of Acts follow Peter's life while the rest of the book zeroes in on Paul's life.

Acts is a very important book for the person who wants to understand the transition from Judaism to Christianity. It also gives us some necessary background to understand the rest of the New Testament. The church grew rapidly at the beginning as the Holy Spirit brought Old Testament believers into the new movement.

During the thirty-year period covered by Acts, the church grew from 120 people to thousands. It spread from an upper room in Jerusalem to an international movement that had followers in most of the Roman Empire and beyond. It changed from a sect of Judaism to include anyone who was willing to follow Jesus, whether they were Jewish or Gentile.

Theme verse: *"But you shall receive power when the Holy Spirit has come upon you; and you shall be witnesses to Me in Jerusalem, and in all Judea and Samaria, and to the end of the earth"* (Acts 1:8).

The Writings of Paul

Romans

Paul wrote this letter to Rome before he visited the city. This was about seven or eight years before the great fire of Rome and the subsequent persecution of Christians.

Someone has said the first eleven chapters of the book of Romans show us how God makes bad people good. The second part of Romans (Chapters 12 to 16) shows us how God makes good people better. The first part is the doctrinal foundation of the Gospel, and the second part is the practical application—showing us how to live the Gospel in everyday life. We could also say Romans shows us how Paul interpreted the life and teachings of Jesus.

Sometimes people call Romans the *Gospel According to Paul.* The main theme of the book is the Gospel, God's plan of salvation for mankind. The theme verses below summarize the message of Romans.

Theme verses: *For I am not ashamed of the gospel of Christ,* *for it is the power of God to salvation for everyone who believes, for the Jew first and also for the Greek. For in it the righteousness of God is revealed from faith to faith; as it is written, "The just shall live by faith"* (Romans 1:16–17).

1 Corinthians

The Corinthian church had a lot of struggles, and they badly needed help. Paul wrote this letter to give them that help. The Corinthian church was in Corinth, a city as sinful as any large American city of today. The members of this church faced daily temptations to yield to the worst sins in existence.

Since this church was new, the members had a lot of questions. They wrote a letter to Paul asking him how to deal with the issues they faced. Here are some of the topics found in this book.

- Divisions in the church (1:12–31)
- Incest (5:1)
- Prostitution (6:16–18)
- Lawsuits between Christians (6:5–7)
- Marriage, remarriage, widows (7)
- Eating food offered to idols (8)
- Head coverings for women (11:2–16)
- The Lord's Supper (11:17–34)

- Prophecy and speaking in tongues (14)
- The resurrection of Christ (15)

Corinth was a divided church with many difficulties, but we see no sign that Paul considered giving up on them. Perhaps his teaching in this book could be summed up like this:

Theme verse: *Therefore, whether you eat or drink, or whatever you do, do all to the glory of God* (1 Corinthians 10:31).

2 Corinthians

Paul visited Corinth after they received his first letter, but he was rejected by some in the church. He left again and wrote a strong letter of rebuke which he sent with Titus. That letter has been lost, but according to 2 Corinthians, the church repented of its attitude toward him and followed his instructions in dealing with the sin among them. Paul wrote 2 Corinthians to assure them of his continued love for them (7:4).

Some members at Corinth accused Paul of being weak in person and only writing strong letters. This led him to explain why it seemed this way. He also affirmed his authority as an apostle (Chapters 10 to 13). We can summarize his feelings toward them like this:

Theme verse: *Therefore I rejoice that I have confidence in you in everything* (2 Corinthians 7:16).

This is the most personal of all Paul's letters. It shares details about Paul's own struggles and the hardships he faced. This gives us an interesting glimpse into Paul's personal life.

Galatians

One commentator says this book shows Paul at his angriest. The church at Galatia had been attacked by the Judaizers, Jewish Christians who followed Paul around on his journeys. They tried to persuade the Gentile converts that they needed to become Jews and live according to the Law of Moses to be saved.

Paul dealt with these ideas very succinctly in this book. But first, he defended his authority as an apostle. The Judaizers probably had persuaded the Galatians that Paul lacked authority to teach salvation by grace. It seems they assumed that anyone who believed in salvation by grace would live a careless and lawless life. Paul addressed these issues as well as the futility of trying to be saved by keeping the Law.

Theme verse: *Stand fast therefore in the liberty by which Christ has made us free, and do not be entangled again with a yoke of bondage* (Galatians 5:1).

Ephesians

The book of Ephesians emphasizes how to act as part of God's family. It is a practical book, one that every Christian should read and pay attention to. The Ephesians were mostly

Gentiles and didn't have a background of walking with God. Paul was careful to assure them that this made no difference. However, as children of God, they had a responsibility to live out what God had called them to.

The book can be divided into two sections:

- Our Calling in Christ (Chapters 1–3)
- Our Walk in Christ (Chapters 4–6)

Theme verses: *I, therefore, the prisoner of the Lord, beseech you to walk worthy of the calling with which you were called, with all lowliness and gentleness, with longsuffering, bearing with one another in love, endeavoring to keep the unity of the Spirit in the bond of peace* (Ephesians 4:1–3).

Philippians

The Philippian church sent a gift to Paul by Epaphroditus. While with Paul in Rome, he became deathly ill. When he finally felt better, Paul sent him home and wrote this letter to send with him. The letter clearly shows Paul's appreciation for the Philippian church.

This is one of Paul's most encouraging letters. Even though the Philippians faced hard times, Paul encouraged them to rejoice. He was a good example for them in this.

Theme verse: *Rejoice in the Lord always. Again I will say, rejoice!* (Philippians 4:4).

Colossians

Paul tended to follow a pattern in his writing. This book again can be divided into two sections. The first two chapters are doctrinal and focus on our identity in Christ. The second section is practical and focuses on our walk in Christ.

Paul had not been to Colossae, but he was concerned that the Christians there would not be misled. False teachers had entered the church and were denying the deity of Jesus. Paul insisted that these teachings were the results of "philosophy and vain deceit" and that "in Him [Christ] dwells all the fullness of the Godhead bodily" (see Colossians 2:8–9).

Theme verses: *As you therefore have received Christ Jesus the Lord, so walk in Him, rooted and built up in Him and established in the faith, as you have been taught, abounding in it with thanksgiving* (Colossians 2:6–7).

1 Thessalonians

Paul had to flee soon after he established the church in Thessalonica. Because of this, he sent Timothy back to check on them. Timothy returned with a good report, so Paul wrote this epistle of commendation and encouragement.[2]

The first part of Chapter 4 deals with living a life pleasing to God. The rest of the book primarily focuses on the Second Coming of Jesus.

---

[2] This is thought to be the first letter Paul wrote.

Theme verse: *Finally then, brethren, we urge and exhort in the Lord Jesus that you should abound more and more, just as you received from us how you ought to walk and to please God* (1 Thessalonians 4:1).

2 Thessalonians

The church in Thessalonica faced several problems Paul needed to address in this letter. It seems some people misunderstood his first letter and had given up their jobs, thinking the Lord was returning soon. Also, false teachers were claiming that Jesus had already returned. According to 2 Thessalonians 2:2, some of these false teachers may have even sent forged letters, claiming they were from Paul.

To top it off, the new church was also facing persecution. Paul reassured them that God would punish their persecutors in His own time.

Theme verse: *But the Lord is faithful, who will establish you and guard you from the evil one* (2 Thessalonians 3:3).

1 Timothy

Paul wrote this book after the end of the book of Acts. He had probably been released from prison, as he had expected (see Philippians 2:24), and had traveled to Ephesus and Philippi. Apparently he left Timothy in charge at Ephesus and later wrote this letter as a follow-up. This book gives us the most detailed instructions for church organization and leadership that we find in the Bible.

Timothy and Paul were close friends, but Timothy was much younger than Paul. This letter shows Paul at his best, mentoring a young man who would replace him after his death.

Theme verse: *I write so that you may know how you ought to conduct yourself in the house of God, which is the church of the living God, the pillar and ground of the truth* (1 Timothy 3:15).

2 Timothy

This letter is thought to be the last one Paul wrote. He was back in Rome in prison. This time, his circumstances were much different from the first time. As you read this book, you can see that Paul was trying to prepare Timothy to go on without him. He had faced many discouragements, and Timothy would face opposition as well. But it is possible to come to the end of life with a testimony like Paul had:

> I have fought the good fight, I have finished the race, I have kept the faith. Finally, there is laid up for me the crown of righteousness, which the Lord, the righteous Judge, will give to me on that Day, and not to me only but also to all who have loved His appearing (2 Timothy 4:7–8).

All of Paul's fellow believers forsook him when he faced Nero this time. But God was with him, and he had the privilege of bringing the Gospel to the most powerful man in Rome. Paul knew the end was near, and he hoped to see Timothy once more before he died (see 4:9). Whether Timothy got there in time, we don't know.

Theme verse: *Hold fast the pattern of sound words which you have heard from me, in faith and love which are in Christ Jesus* (2 Timothy 1:13).

Titus

Paul had left Titus on the island of Crete around the same time he left Timothy in Ephesus. He gave Titus a similar commission. In this letter, Paul instructs Titus how to handle the special challenges of the Cretan culture.

The first step was to appoint leaders. In Chapter 1, Paul clearly lays out the qualifications for potential leaders. In Chapter 2, he lays out a teaching plan to help the Cretans overcome the shortcomings of their culture. And finally, in the last chapter, Paul states the need for Christians to live godly lives.

Theme verse: *For this reason I left you in Crete, that you should set in order the things that are lacking, and appoint elders in every city as I commanded you* (Titus 1:5).

Philemon

Philemon provides an interesting example of living for Christ in real life. Philemon was a slave owner. His runaway slave, Onesimus, had met Paul, and Paul led him to faith in Christ. Now what? Onesimus had some restitution to make with his master. And Philemon had the legal right to deal out severe punishment. But the two men had become brothers in Christ.

Paul wrote some pointed personal advice to Philemon. The letter was also public and meant to be read to the whole church. Here we see the clash of cultures that can take place when people become Christians.

Theme verses: *For perhaps he departed for a while for this purpose, that you might receive him forever, no longer as a slave but more than a slave—a beloved brother, especially to me but how much more to you, both in the flesh and in the Lord* (Philemon 15–16).

The General Epistles

This is the "other" section of the New Testament. It is a group of epistles accepted by the church as inspired, but not written by Paul. The first one, Hebrews, is in a strategic position. It is either at the end of the writings of Paul or at the beginning of the writings of others. The author of Hebrews is a bit of a mystery. Some scholars feel Paul wrote it; others feel he didn't. Putting it here in the

New Testament was the one solution both camps could agree with.

Hebrews

We don't know who wrote this book, but the author was well versed in the Old Testament. For instance, over half of the verses in the first chapter contain quotes from the Old Testament. The writer also assumed his readers knew the Old Testament, especially the writings of Moses.

This book is an in-depth theological presentation of the superiority of Jesus over the angels, Moses, Joshua, and the Old Testament priesthood. This is the foundation of the book's contention that the new covenant of Christ is superior to the old covenant presented in the Old Testament.

Theme verses: *Let us hold fast the confession of our hope without wavering, for He who promised is faithful. And let us consider one another in order to stir up love and good works* (Hebrews 10:23–24).

James

The book of James was written to Jews and emphasizes the importance of good works to prove our faith. Like today, some Christians back then thought that if they were under grace, their works no longer mattered. James disagreed strongly. He wrote that "faith without works is dead." He also said, "Show me your faith without your works, and I will show you my faith by my works."

This book should be required reading for everyone who claims to be a Christian. Today's young people are sick of the hypocrisy of Christians who have lots to say about being saved but live no differently from the sinners around them.

Theme verse: *But be doers of the word, and not hearers only, deceiving yourselves* (James 1:22).

1 Peter

Persecution was coming. Peter wrote this around the time of the great fire of Rome that triggered the first major persecution of Christians. Peter, like Paul, was executed during this period of oppression.

The focus of this book is accepting suffering. Peter's big concern was that our Christian testimony would cause the oppressors to glorify God.

Theme verse: *Yet if anyone suffers as a Christian, let him not be ashamed, but let him glorify God in this matter* (1 Peter 4:16).

2 Peter

This was Peter's last letter and his last message to the church of Christ. Like other Bible writers, he was concerned that God's people would remain faithful after he was gone. He warned against false teachers and mockers who would discredit the idea of Jesus' return.

The last part of this letter is similar to the letter Jude wrote.

Theme verses: *Beloved, I now write to you this second epistle (in both of which I stir up your pure minds by way of reminder), that you may be mindful of the words which were spoken before by the holy prophets, and of the commandment of us, the apostles of the Lord and Savior* (2 Peter 3:1–2).

1 John

It seems John did his writing toward the end of his life. He looked around at the churches and saw their struggles. In this letter, he writes about some things that would help them draw closer to God and resist false teaching.

John was a logical writer. He saw life in black and white. He separated right and wrong and didn't leave any gray areas between them. He also used parallels and contrasts to make his points: "Christ vs. antichrists, light vs. darkness, truth vs. falsehood, righteousness vs. sin, love of the Father vs. love of the world, and the Spirit of God vs. the spirit of the Antichrist."[3]

- This book emphasizes the evidence of love.
- If you love God, you will keep His commandments.
- If you love God, you will love the children of God.
- You can't love God and hate your fellow man.

---

[3] http://www.insight.org/resources/bible/the-general-epistles/first-john

- God is love, and therefore love will be a sign that we are His children.

Theme verse: *And this is His commandment: that we should believe on the name of His Son Jesus Christ and love one another, as He gave us commandment* (1 John 3:23).

2 John

This was a personal letter from John to "the elect lady and her children."[4] He defined the relationship between love and the truth (vv. 1, 2), between truth and obedience (v. 4), and between obedience and love (v. 5).

In the latter part of this short letter, he warned against taking a soft approach toward false teachers.

Theme verse: *This is love, that we walk according to His commandments. This is the commandment, that as you have heard from the beginning, you should walk in it* (2 John 6).

3 John

This was another personal letter John wrote to a man named Gaius. At that time, the churches sent out evangelists to preach the Gospel. In the church where Gaius was, a leader called Diotrephes refused to welcome the evangelists. He

---

[4] This could have been a family member, or it could have been a euphemism for a church he was writing to.

even excommunicated people who showed hospitality to them. He also rejected a letter John had written, perhaps as an introduction to the evangelists. In 3 John, John commended Gaius for his faithfulness and assured him that he would deal with Diotrephes when he visited.

Theme verse: *I have no greater joy than to hear that my children walk in truth* (3 John 4).

Jude

Jude had a desire to write about the good news of the Gospel, but he felt compelled to write about the false teachers threatening the church. Parts of this letter are similar to portions of 2 Peter. After his denunciation of the false prophets who had crept in secretly, Jude offered some solutions and ended on a positive note.

Theme verse: *Beloved, while I was very diligent to write to you concerning our common salvation, I found it necessary to write to you exhorting you to contend earnestly for the faith which was once for all delivered to the saints* (Jude 3).

Apocalyptic Writing

Revelation

This final book of the Bible is an example of apocalyptic writing. The writer used symbolism and word pictures to tell his story. John wrote this book while he was exiled to Patmos, an island in the Aegean Sea.

The first chapters of the book contain messages from Jesus to the seven churches of Asia Minor. These messages are a concise evaluation of the spiritual condition of each church. These evaluations range from total approval to complete disapproval.

Chapters 4 to 18 cover the battle between good and evil on earth. Some scholars consider this part of the book to have been fulfilled at the fall of Jerusalem. Others feel it reviews the history of good and evil several times, and still others believe most of the events described will happen in the future.

Chapters 19 to 22 show the final triumph of good over evil and picture life after the battle is over.

Theme verse: *"Write the things which you have seen, and the things which are, and the things which will take place after this"* (Revelation 1:19).

6

Reading the Bible

There are many ways to read a book. However, you will soon learn that the Bible is a one-of-a-kind book that requires its own approach. It contains many stories, but reading the Bible isn't like reading a novel. It teaches us many things, but it isn't a textbook. It documents history, but it isn't just a history book either.

The following sections will give you some suggestions to help you get the most value for your reading time.

When You Read . . .

Be Systematic
One of the worst ways to read the Bible is the "hit or miss"

method. If you just grab your Bible each day and let it fall open and read a few random verses, you will not learn to understand it. You need a reading plan that will help you to understand what you are reading.

A new reader, starting to learn about the Bible, should start with the Gospels. The Gospel of Matthew is a good one, since it comes first. Then continue to read through all four of the Gospels. By then you will have a better idea of who Jesus is and why He came to earth. At that point you might want to go back and reread the Gospels. Things that seemed obscure the first time will make more sense as you read again.

After the Gospels, you should read the book of Acts. This will give you the story of what happened after Jesus' resurrection and tell how the Gospel spread throughout Israel and all the way to Rome.

Then try some of the shorter epistles. First John is a good one to start with. As you read the epistles, you will learn more about applying Jesus' teachings in everyday life. Probably books like Romans and Hebrews will be harder for you, but even the longer epistles like 1 Corinthians will help you learn about practical Christian living. Many of the epistles were letters written by apostles to help solve problems people were facing. As you read, you will discover that people haven't changed that much, and what was applicable two thousand years ago is still relevant today.

Look for the Main Idea

The Bible wasn't written to entertain an audience. You will find that what it contains is there for a reason. But some of those reasons are more important than others. For instance, in Matthew 13:1–9 Jesus told a simple story about a man who was planting a field. Since Jesus wasn't just making small talk, we can assume He was teaching some truth in this story (this kind of story is called a parable).

To find the truth Jesus was teaching, we need to look for the main idea. Let's look at the story and try to picture the scene. When a farmer planted a field in those days, he took a bag of seed to the field and walked back and forth, scattering the seed by hand.

As you read the story, you will notice that some of the seed landed on a pathway beside the field and the birds ate it. Some fell on a stony part of the field, where the topsoil was shallow. The seed sprouted and grew quickly, but then it died because it couldn't produce good roots. Some fell in a weedy, thorny area and was choked out by the weeds. But some of the seed landed on the good soil where the farmer wanted it. But even in the good soil, some parts of the field had a better crop than others.

So, what was Jesus saying? In this case, He explained the meaning of the parable to His disciples afterward. You can find His explanation later in the same chapter (vv. 18–23).

First, the seed was the Word of God. Someone was telling people the good news of the Gospel, but not everyone responded in the same way. The pathway represented people who didn't understand and weren't interested. They ignored the message, and the devil made sure they forgot it.

The stony place with shallow topsoil represented people who were glad to hear the message, but when they received opposition, they soon abandoned the ideas they had heard.

The thorny ground represented people who were so busy making money and looking after their possessions that they quickly forgot what they had heard.

Finally, the good ground represented people who were interested in the gospel message. They received it gladly and let it grow in their lives. While some of them understood it better and produced more fruit than others, all of them become productive followers of God.

The key to understanding this story is to identify the main ideas. The seed in this parable represents the Gospel, and the ground shows us different kinds of people. Once you realize some of these basic facts, the story begins to make sense.

Taking your time when you read will aid your search for the main idea. Read a section at a time and figure out what it is talking about. Reread it as often as you need to. You don't need to pass any speed-reading tests, and you don't need to read the Bible from cover to cover four times a year, like a friend of mine does. Once you get the main idea of the parable, it is much more interesting than it was when it seemed to be nothing more than a story about a farmer planting a field.

This idea refers to more than just the stories in the Bible. We can look at a passage like John 3:1–15 for another example. Nicodemus came to Jesus to ask Him some questions. Jesus told him that unless a person is born again, he can't see the kingdom of God. This didn't make any sense to Nicodemus because he didn't know what Jesus was referring to. Surely Jesus didn't mean he was to become a baby again and be born as he was the first time.

No, Jesus was talking about a different birth. Nicodemus's first birth was when he was born as a human being, made of flesh. The second birth would be when he was born as a spiritual baby.

When you read the Bible, you will stumble over many places that seem hard to figure out. But always look for the main idea. If you can figure out the central truth, the rest of the passage will usually fall into place.

Figure Out the Author's Perspective

A book of the Bible will make more sense to you if you know

where the writer was coming from and what he was after. As you read, try to answer the following basic questions.

- Is the writer speaking in allegories that you need to figure out? The book of Revelation speaks about a beast with nine heads and ten horns. The writer explains that the ten horns are ten kings, which indicates he is writing in word pictures, or allegories. Revelation will not make sense to you if you read it like one of the Gospels, that is, a simple history of what happened.

- What is the author's background? The author of the book of James was a converted Pharisee and had a strong Jewish background. When he wrote the book of James, he spoke from this perspective. Luke, however, was a converted Gentile doctor, so we would expect his perspective to be a lot different from James's.

- Who is the author's intended audience? Luke tells you he is writing to Theopholis, a converted Roman Gentile. James says he is writing to dispersed Jews. Naturally, Luke's writing will be different from James's. James can take for granted that his readers understand some things Luke's readers don't.

Your Bible may give you some of this information. If not, a simple Bible dictionary will tell you about it. But even without a Bible dictionary, you can often determine the author's perspective from what he says. Pay special attention to the introduction because it often contains some simple facts that will help you to understand the book better.

A few of the Bible writers were well educated. Paul, for instance, had a background in Jewish theology and had trained under Gamaliel, a leading Jewish rabbi. Books like Romans show Paul's theological understanding and academic background. But he had also learned to understand people. Many of his letters were written to solve problems, and he knew how to build bridges with people. But even in the letters that focus on problem-solving, Paul often starts by laying a doctrinal foundation and ends by making practical applications to everyday life.

On the other hand, many of the writers of the Bible were just ordinary people. Peter and John, unlike Paul, had minimal education. The Pharisees called them ignorant and unlearned. Naturally, their writings seem more "homespun." They also seem more practical than the theological books.

You will learn some of these things as you become more acquainted with the Bible. To start with, you will probably feel more comfortable with the practical writings than with epistles like Romans and Hebrews.

Understand the Context

The Bible has been used to justify some bizarre ideas. Often this is because people do not take the time to understand the context of the verses upon which the claim is based. A good way to avoid this is to read the context of a verse that is puzzling you. This will often clarify its meaning. Note that the context can vary, depending on the situation. Look for the change of thought before and after the passage you are looking at, and study the entire section your passage is in. In other cases, the context might be the entire chapter. Context could also include parallel passages in other places in the Bible.

Another important thing to remember is that we should always interpret difficult or obscure verses in light of clear teaching elsewhere. For instance, Luke 14:26 says, "If anyone comes to Me and does not hate his father and mother, wife and children, brothers and sisters, yes, and his own life also, he cannot be My disciple." That sounds very strange at first. It doesn't even seem right. But Matthew 10:37 says it like this: "He who loves father or mother more than Me is not worthy of Me. And he who loves son or daughter more than Me is not worthy of Me." The verse in Matthew explains what Jesus meant in Luke.[1]

---

[1] This has to do with Hebrew expressions. (Hebrew tended to use exaggeration rather than adjectives and adverbs to make a point.) Luke, because of his precision in writing history, probably gave the exact quotation. Matthew, however, gave an indirect quotation which clarified the meaning of what Jesus said. This approach was perfectly acceptable in the Eastern mindset and would not have been viewed as a contradiction.

As I said earlier, some of these things will become easier with practice. Don't give up too quickly. If you don't understand something, keep on reading. Come back another day and reread it or talk to a friend about it. Discussing a passage with someone else often helps to clarify it.

Take Notes

If you really want to remember something you have read, write it down. You may want to have a notebook and record your questions about verses you encounter. Write down truths that strike you as significant. Some people use a highlighter to mark such passages. Do whatever works well for you.

A while ago, I decided to study a single book of the Bible. I printed it from a Bible program on my computer. Then I listened to the book from an audio Bible while following along on the printed copy. I repeated this probably a dozen times, highlighting positive statements in one color and negative statements in a different one. I highlighted questions in still another color. I jotted questions I wanted to explore further in the margin. I circled important words and wrote comments in the margin.

It was amazing how much this exercise helped me understand the meaning of the book.

You might not find this as helpful as I did. Perhaps you want to read out loud to yourself. You will find many ways to explore a piece of writing, and none of them are wrong. You will gradually find the ways you are comfortable with.

More Ways to Read the Bible

Once you get used to reading the Bible you may want to expand a bit.

Studying a Book

When you study a book of the Bible, you will want to take notes. Jot down the author, his background, his frame of reference, and his audience. This will help you to understand the book. Read it carefully several times, maybe even in several different translations. This will broaden your understanding.

Try to write an outline of the book. You will find outlines in various Bible helps, but they will vary. Coming up with your own outline will force you to evaluate and understand what the book is saying.

Write down your thoughts and questions. These things are helpful to understand what you are reading.

If you really want to understand what you are reading, teach a Bible study class on the book. I never really enjoyed or understood the Minor Prophets until I taught a Sunday school class based on them. Teaching and discussion go a long way to helping you understand.

Studying a Person

Another interesting approach to the Bible is to do a character study. Of course, you have been studying the life of Jesus just by reading the Gospels. But try studying some of the Old Testament characters like Abraham, Joseph, Samson, or David. You will definitely learn things from each of these men's lives.

To do a proper study of a Bible character, you will want to read everything the Bible says about him or her. If you are studying Samson, be sure to also read what the New Testament says about him. Reading what Hebrews 11 says about him may change your perception of him a little.

Studying a Subject

Topical studies are very common in churches today. Many sermons are topical and consist of picking out verses throughout the Bible that help us to understand the subject. Some basic tools, like a topical Bible, will help with this.

Remember, however, to be honest when you study a subject. Don't start with your conclusions and then try to verify them. Instead, let the Bible speak for itself.

The scientific method works for Bible study. If you want to do a topical study, start with a question. Then clarify the question by narrowing it down to something you can handle. For instance, don't try to study a subject called "The

Church" or "The Bible." Cut it down to one segment of the subject. For instance, take the question, "Why should I read the Bible?"

The next step is gathering your data. Find all the Bible verses that apply to your question. Read them, classify them, and try to understand all the different angles. Use your Bible's center column cross references to find other verses that apply.

After you have become well acquainted with the Bible's teaching on your subject, try to outline it. Outlining is a basic skill that does a lot to enhance a student's comprehension. You should be able to come up with some tentative conclusions, but continue to test your ideas. Ask other people about them. Explain how you came up with them. Defend them! But always be open for more data to add to your study and more angles from which to approach it.

7

Where Did the Bible Come From?

Some people treat the Bible as they would any other ancient book. In fact, where the Bible disagrees with another writing, they usually assume the Bible is wrong. Often the other book will have been written hundreds of years after the fact, so to level things out, critics search the Bible for clues that would indicate its writings were written by people who assumed the name of a Bible character.

This is especially true where the Biblical writers wrote prophecies that were later fulfilled. Critics assume that such prophecy must have been written after the fact.[1]

Written by Men but Inspired by God

The Bible was written by real people. Many of them identified themselves when they wrote or were identified as the authors by others. In fact, this has always been one of the tests of canonicity for both the Old Testament and the New Testament.

My inclination is to not take the insinuations of higher criticism too seriously. Most of them are the product of spiritual cynics who do not believe in the inspiration of the Bible. They are looking for evidence to support their position. Other people, just as educated and just as intelligent, have spent most of their lives studying the ideas of higher criticism and refuting them.

This is not to say that every idea raised by a critic must be wrong. Textual criticism[2] has a place in identifying the correct text of the Bible. But we shouldn't be the first ones standing in line to accept every new idea that surfaces, because many don't stand the test of time and closer examination.

The idea of inspiration hits a lot of people wrong, partly

---

[1] This is speaking of higher criticism, not textual criticism. Higher criticism is very subjective in nature.

[2] Often called lower criticism, as opposed to the higher criticism we have been looking at. Lower criticism can be valuable, but higher criticism seldom is.

because this implies authority. Higher criticism goes to great lengths to avoid admitting that God inspired the Bible.

What do we mean when we say the Bible was inspired? Paul addressed this in 2 Timothy 3:16. "All Scripture is given by inspiration of God, and is profitable for doctrine, for reproof, for correction, for instruction in righteousness, that the man of God may be complete, thoroughly equipped for every good work."

The word *inspiration* literally means "breathed out." In fact, one translation says, "All Scripture is breathed out by God . . ."[3] This concept is hard to explain. It doesn't mean God dictated the Bible word for word. God used men to write the Bible, and these men had personalities, along with individual strengths and weaknesses. God worked within this framework of imperfect people to bring His Word to humanity as we have it today in the Bible.

Most Christians have experienced times when God gave them words they needed in a discussion with someone. Later they looked back at that and wondered where those words came from. The concept of inspiration worked like this. You can find another illustration in Luke 12:11–12: "Now when they bring you to the synagogues and magistrates and authorities, do not worry about how or what you

---

[3] The English Standard Version (ESV).

should answer, or what you should say. For the Holy Spirit will teach you in that very hour what you ought to say."

This doesn't mean our words at such a time have the same authority the Bible has, but it is an example of how the process worked. In many cases, the writers might not even have realized they were writing inspired Scripture.

The Bible Is God's Word

The Bible tells us clearly that it is inspired by God. In other words, it is God's message to us. If this is true, then we had better pay attention to it. God's standard is a high one. In fact, if we haven't committed our lives to Him and tapped into His power, it is an impossible standard. With His help, we can live for Him. However, we will never get to the place where we have learned everything God has for us. The Bible is one of our lifelines to God. We seldom open it without learning something else about Him or ourselves.

Rightly Dividing God's Word

The difference between the Old and New Testament can be confusing to new readers. The Bible is a progressive revelation of God's message. In the Garden of Eden, God walked and talked with Adam and Eve. They didn't need a special revelation to know God because He was right there with them. But all that changed when they sinned.

At first, God approached godly men on a personal level, but never to the extent that He had approached Adam and Eve. For instance, He spoke to Enoch and to Noah. Later He spoke to Abraham and to Moses. That was the first level of revelation.

From the time of Moses, God approached His people as a nation. He gave Moses laws to guide them. These laws revealed many things God's people had not known before. For instance, God clarified in the Law that a man should not marry his sister or a closely related woman. But Abraham's wife, Sarah, was Abraham's half sister. God had not revealed this prohibition in Abraham's time.

The knowledge of God kept growing throughout the Old Testament. God told them in the Law they needed to offer sacrifices for their sins. But later He told them He wanted more than that. He wanted them to have repentant hearts. In the Sermon on the Mount, Jesus enlarged on this. It was no longer enough to just avoid committing adultery; God also expected a man to remain pure in his thoughts and not to lust after a woman.

The final revelation from God was the New Testament. God's plan for restoring His fellowship with people culminated in Jesus, who taught God's revelation. He lived it as well. As people watched Him and listened to His teaching, they learned more about God than anyone had ever known before.

Later Jesus died, providing the ultimate sacrifice for our sins. Finally, after His resurrection, He sent the Holy Spirit to live in the hearts of those who committed themselves to Him. Today, you can fellowship with God in a way unknown to the Old Testament followers of God. The Holy Spirit will interpret God's message to you as you read the Bible. He will carry your message to God as you pray. He will put God's thoughts in your mind when you pray for wisdom.

The whole Bible deserves to be read. But because of this progressive revelation from God, we find our primary guidance for life from the New Testament. If you read the Sermon on the Mount in Matthew 5–7, you will see the comparisons Jesus made between the Old Testament teachings and the teachings He was bringing into the New Testament.

And Finally . . .

Someday we will meet God face to face. I'm not sure if Adam and Eve ever saw God or not. They may have merely felt His presence and heard His voice. But in the last chapters of Revelation, you can read about a future time when we will see God and Jesus face to face. That will be glorious!

The New Testament also gives us a beautiful picture of the kingdom of heaven on earth. This kingdom calls us to unselfish service for Christ. We don't give our hearts to Jesus just to escape hellfire. We receive Him as our Lord and Master and live in obedience to Him so that He will be glorified on earth. We can be part of that kingdom, here and now, as well as in the future.

As you take the time to read the Bible, the Word of God, may you understand the invitation God extends to you. It is an invitation to surrender your life to Him and become part of His kingdom here on the earth. Then, as a citizen of the kingdom of heaven, you will have power to live according to God's will and a desire to invite others to join it as well.

About the Author

Lester Bauman was born into an Old Order Mennonite home close to Kitchener, Ontario. Later, his family joined a local conservative Mennonite church. As a young-married man, he taught for five years in several Christian schools. He then worked for thirteen years out of a home office for Rod and Staff Publishers, Inc. as a writer and editor. During this time, he and his wife Marlene moved with their family from Ontario to Alberta, where they live presently. They have six children and ten grandchildren, and are members of a local Western Fellowship Mennonite Church.

During his time with Rod and Staff, Lester wrote ten books, including *The True Christian* and *God and Uncle Dale,* both available from Christian Aid Ministries. He spent a number of years in Alberta working as an HR manager in a corporate setting. He now works for the Christian Aid Ministries billboard evangelism ministry out of a home office, doing content writing for their website, answering correspondence, and serving as the phone team "encourager."

Lester recently self-published a book based on Ecclesiastes titled, *Where Is God When Life Doesn't Make Sense*. He is also working on several books for Christian Aid Ministries as he has time.

You can contact Lester through his personal website at www.lbauman.ca or by email at lester.bauman@gmail.com. You may also write to him in care of Christian Aid Ministries, P.O. Box 360, Berlin, Ohio 44610.

About Christian Aid Ministries

Christian Aid Ministries was founded in 1981 as a nonprofit, tax-exempt 501(c)(3) organization. Its primary purpose is to provide a trustworthy and efficient channel for Amish, Mennonite, and other conservative Anabaptist groups and individuals to minister to physical and spiritual needs around the world. This is in response to the command to ". . . do good unto all men, especially unto them who are of the household of faith" (Galatians 6:10).

Each year, CAM supporters provide 15-20 million pounds of food, clothing, medicines, seeds, Bibles, Bible story books, and other Christian literature for needy people. Most of the aid goes to orphans and Christian families. Supporters' funds also help to clean up and rebuild for natural disaster victims, put up Gospel billboards in the U.S., support several church-planting efforts, operate two medical clinics, and provide resources for needy families to make their own living. CAM's main purposes for providing aid are to help and encourage God's people and bring the Gospel to a lost and dying world.

CAM has staff, warehouses, and distribution networks in Romania, Moldova, Ukraine, Haiti, Nicaragua, Liberia, Israel, and Kenya. Aside from management, supervisory personnel, and bookkeeping operations, volunteers do most of the work at CAM locations. Each year, volunteers at our warehouses, field bases, Disaster Response Services projects, and other locations donate over 200,000 hours of work.

CAM's ultimate purpose is to glorify God and help enlarge His kingdom. ". . . whatsoever ye do, do all to the glory of God" (1 Corinthians 10:31).

The Way to God and Peace

We live in a world contaminated by sin. Sin is anything that goes against God's holy standards. When we do not follow the guidelines that God our Creator gave us, we are guilty of sin. Sin separates us from God, the source of life.

Since the time when the first man and woman, Adam and Eve, sinned in the Garden of Eden, sin has been universal. The Bible says that we all have "sinned and come short of the glory of God" (Romans 3:23). It also says that the natural consequence for that sin is eternal death, or punishment in an eternal hell: "Then when lust hath conceived, it bringeth forth sin: and sin, when it is finished, bringeth forth death" (James 1:15).

But we do not have to suffer eternal death in hell. God provided a sacrifice for our sins through the gift of His only Son,

Jesus Christ. "For God so loved the world that he gave his only begotten Son, that whosoever believeth in him should not perish, but have everlasting life" (John 3:16).

A sacrifice is something given to benefit someone else. It costs the giver greatly. Jesus was God's sacrifice. Jesus' death takes away the penalty of sin for all those who accept this sacrifice and truly repent of their sins. To repent of sins means to be truly sorry for and turn away from the things we have done that have violated God's standards (Acts 2:38; 3:19).

Jesus died, but He did not remain dead. After three days, God's Spirit miraculously raised Him to life again. God's Spirit does something similar in us. When we receive Jesus as our sacrifice and repent of our sins, our hearts are changed. We become spiritually alive! We develop new desires and attitudes (2 Corinthians 5:17). We begin to make choices that please God (1 John 3:9). If we do fail and commit sins, we can ask God for forgiveness. "If we confess our sins, he is faithful and just to forgive us our sins, and to cleanse us from all unrighteousness" (1 John 1:9).

Once our hearts have been changed, we want to continue growing spiritually. We will be happy to let Jesus be the Master of our lives and will want to become more like Him. To do this, we must meditate on God's Word and commune with God in prayer. We will testify to others of this change by being baptized and sharing the good news of God's victory over sin and death. Fellowship with a faithful group of believers will strengthen our walk with God (1 John 1:7).